Leisure Arts 44
Painting
Garden Plants
in Watercolour
Kathleen Stroud

SEARCH PRESS

Introduction

I was brought up surrounded by the beautiful garden which my father created, so I suppose it was inevitable that sooner or later I would develop some interest in the flowers and plants which grew in such abundance around me.

Since childhood my paintings and drawings have always been extremely detailed. At school I remember my art teacher telling me to go home and draw a cooker, presumably with the idea of encouraging me to paint more imaginatively and thus more fluidly – it did not work! Kitchen implements produced no emotion in me whatsoever. A painting can be as detailed or as abstract as you like, but without some sort of emotion and depth of feeling from its creator, it will always lack 'life'. For my art 'O' Level I chose the *Clematis montana* as my subject, and from then onwards I was hooked on painting plants. So began the wonderful challenge of colour and texture which I find so exciting.

The Chinese and Japanese have traditionally practised a somewhat stylized method of painting flowers. By using economical motifs they portray in a masterly fashion the essence of flowers with a few simple strokes of the brush. In the West, however, the approach has generally been more naturalistic. Originally it was the medicinal powers of wild plants which prompted people to study them; hence the need for close attention to detail. There was also considerable interest in flowers and herbs in the Elizabethan era. The eighteenth century was the heyday of the flower painter, producing such distinguished names as Georg Ehret, Pierre Joseph Redouté, the Bauer brothers, and Pierre Jean Turpin, to name a few. By the nineteenth century, botany was a favourite pastime and young ladies often spent their leisure time painting flowers.

Today, flowers and fruits remain as popular a subject as ever, and their ready availability make them the ideal subject for both professional and aspiring artists. The wealth of subject-matter they provide is infinite. Masses of new varieties and specimens are continually appearing on the market, and my annual visit to the Chelsea Flower Show or the Royal Horticultural Show never fails to make my heart leap with excitement.

Friends and neighbours have been very good in providing me with any plants, flowers, and vegetables which I do not have growing in my garden. Of course, the countryside is also an excellent source of wild flowers, although you should take care not to pick protected species. Remember that wild flowers are far more delicate than most cultivated plants and do not last long in water once picked, so you will have to capture your subject quickly before it starts to wilt. Similarly, fruits have a limited lifespan and need capturing on paper as quickly as possible.

In this book I hope to encourage you to share some of my enthusiasm for the plants, flowers, herbs, and fruits which grow in the garden. Once you start to look at plants really closely your natural curiosity will urge you to find out more: how plants are structured; how and where they grow; how they are fertilized, flower, fruit, and die. Look around you – and then look again. Search for the unexpected and the surprising; observe the changes in colours and textures. Study the blossoms in May; the heavy boughs of ripened fruit in summer; the peas swelling in their pods. Look at the subtle greens of herbs and try to make the crushed scent of them almost rise up from the page by use of colour. Look carefully, and you will find that the garden can be an exciting source of painting material as well as a constant source of pleasure and culinary delights all the year round.

Materials and equipment

Generally, you will find that it pays in the long run to buy materials and equipment of the best quality you can afford.

Paints

As my work often requires extremely delicate washes of colour, I try always to use colours that do not fade. I use both pans and tubes of paint, mixed on a white palette. Colour plays such a crucial part in the accurate portrayal of plants that I make certain that the colours mixed on the palette are correct before applying them to paper. I then test each colour on a rough sheet of paper identical to that I intend using for the final painting, as the different absorbency levels of paper can affect colours. I change the water regularly to keep the colours as fresh and pure as possible.

The colours I use most often are rose madder, cadmium red pale, carmine, scarlet lake, vermilion, lemon yellow, spectrum yellow, gamboge yellow, raw umber, burnt sienna, Vandyke brown, sap green, leaf green, Hooker's green, ultramarine blue, Prussian blue, purple lake, ivory black, and designer gouache white.

Pencils

I generally use HB pencils for my initial drawings, but sometimes I use a softer 3B pencil.

Papers

The paper I use varies according to the subject; delicate wild plants demand a smoother surface than that I would choose for the flamboyant poppy, for example. Generally it tends to be a 180gsm (90lb) watercolour paper with a slight tooth. The style of my work requires very few watery washes. This means that cockling is not a problem, so I rarely need to stretch the paper.

I always use acid-free paper and mounting board to ensure as little deterioration as possible.

Brushes

For detailed painting I use Nos. 000 and 00000 sable brushes. (With detailed work of this kind, I find that they generally only last for up to four completed works!) I also use Nos. 3, 2, and 1 for washes.

Technique

As with most painting subjects, there is a sense of urgency when painting plants, the lifespan of most flowers and vegetables being such that it is difficult to paint the whole group or bunch in detail in one go. I start by deciding what I want to paint; for example, a selection of spring flowers. I gather these from the garden and put them in a vase of water. I do not attempt to draw the whole bunch at once, but select one which I hope to make the focal point of the picture, and place this in a specimen vase, approximately 60cm (24in) away from me.

My work grows as it goes along. In this way I find that I can renew my supply of flowers as I go, without having captured the entire original bunch in pencil only to find that half of them have wilted or died by the time I come to paint them! I tend to work from the centre outwards and upwards, resting my hand on a piece of paper to avoid marks or smudging. Mistakes in the drawing are corrected with an ordinary eraser, although I use a putty eraser when working on textured paper to avoid damaging the surface. I work with my paper flat on the table – this is contrary to what one is generally taught and is purely a personal preference – and with the light coming from the window to my left.

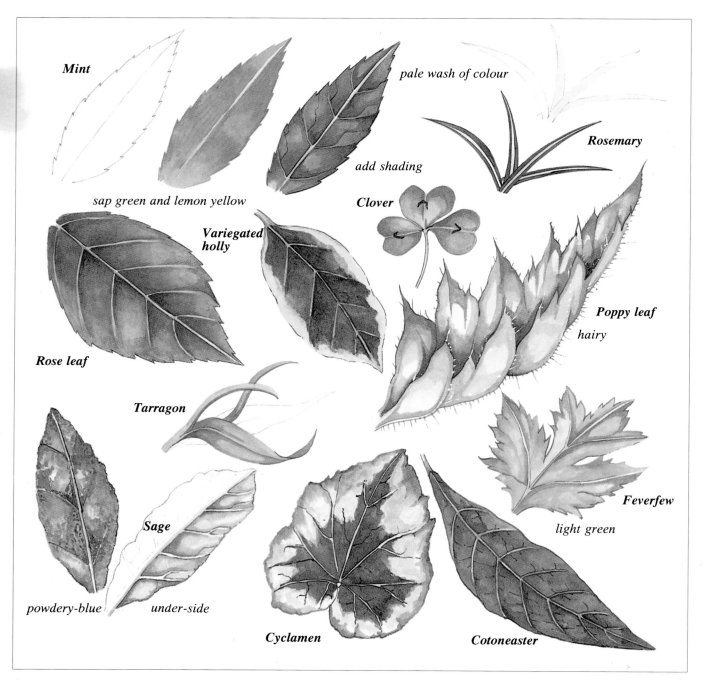

Mint

pale wash of colour

add shading

Rosemary

sap green and lemon yellow

Clover

Variegated holly

Poppy leaf

hairy

Rose leaf

Tarragon

Feverfew

light green

Sage

powdery-blue   *under-side*

Cyclamen

Cotoneaster

Opposite: I have painted these leaves to demonstrate the infinite variety of beautiful and fascinating shapes, textures, and colours that can be found in even a small garden.

Leeks: demonstration

Original size: 29 x 33cm (11½ x 13¼in)
Paper: Saunders Waterford Series, 180gsm (90lb) HP
Brushes: Nos. 2, 1, 000, and 00000 sable

At first sight the leek does not appear to have sufficient variation in colour to be visually exciting to the artist, but on closer study you will discover its many variations of green and some interesting textures. The structure of a leek is beautiful, with its sturdy thick leaves and long body tapering into delicate roots.

Once the leek has been pulled from the allotment or vegetable patch it can be replanted in the garden to keep it fresh until you are ready to begin painting. Unlike many other plants, once the leek has been pulled up it will last quite a long time before showing signs of wilting, so there is not the usual frantic rush to paint it before it dies.

Stage 1

Stage 1

Firstly, I position the leek in front of me, balanced upright with a vase behind for support. Then I draw the leek faintly in pencil before laying the first pale wash of colour – sap green, lemon yellow, Hooker's green, and ultramarine blue. The roots are washed with a mixture of Vandyke brown, carmine, and lemon yellow.

Stage 2 (overleaf)

After the initial wash of colour has dried, I begin to build up the shading on the leaves of the leek. Sit and look carefully at your subject, noticing not only where the darker colours appear, but

Stage 2

Stage 3

appear, but also where the darkest tones are. I use a mixture of viridian, Prussian blue, and lemon yellow to shade the base of the leaves and where the leaves bend over.

Stage 3

Concentrating now on the body of the leek, I darken the colour slightly using sap green and lemon yellow mixed with a hint of ultramarine blue. On top of this, with a more concentrated mixture of sap green and ultramarine blue, I begin to draw the delicate lines on the stem of the leeks with vertical brush strokes from bottom to top. I outline the roots with a faint hint

of scarlet lake mixed with raw umber and a touch of black, shading slightly more at the top of the root.

To finish the study I add the details to the leek, using my finest No. 00000 brush. I emphasize the different lines and deep shadows with sap green and ultramarine blue, and edge the cut-off ends of the leek with Vandyke brown. The base of the leek is painted with Prussian blue mixed with lemon yellow and black to create the shading of one white end against another, and the roots are re-emphasized to help them to stand out.

Stage 4 – the finished painting

Building up a still-life group of three leeks, I arrange them so that I can make the most of their marvellous green leaves at one end and their delicate roots at the other. It is interesting painting the mass of green leaves, laying greens on top of greens and building up tones and shapes using the same colours. Here it is important to move the brush fluidly in the direction of growth. A larger No. 2 brush is used here for the broader washes of pigment.

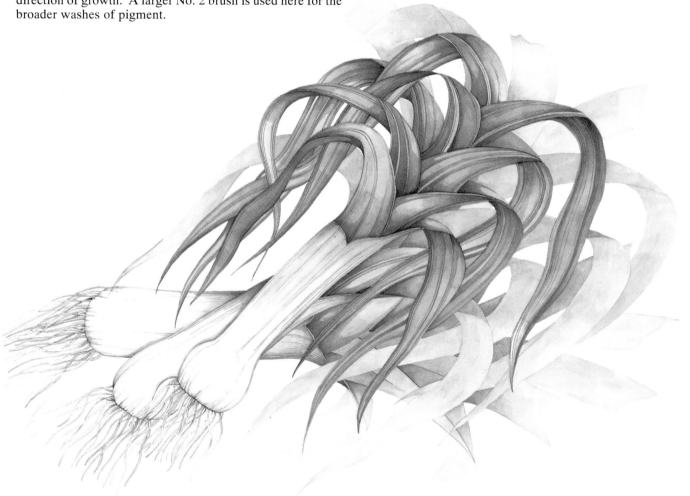

Stage 4 – the finished painting

Runner bean

Original size: 35.5 x 30.5cm (14¼ x 12¼in)
Paper: Whatman hot-pressed, 300gsm (140lb)
Brushes: Nos. 2, 1, 000, and 00000 sable

Runner beans may not readily spring to mind as a painting subject, but you will be amazed at what wonderfully vivid colouring they can provide; the juxtaposition of complementary colours cannot fail to ensure a vibrant combination of red and green. The runner bean is also a joy compositionally, with leaves and flowers that intertwine lovingly in a jumble of twisting forms.

I draw the subject with a sharp HB pencil, then begin to lay in the transparent wash of colour on the leaves with a No. 2 brush, using a weak mixture of sap green and lemon yellow. For the under-side of the leaf I mix pale sap green with lemon yellow and ultramarine blue. The flowers consist of vermilion mixed with gamboge yellow, which I apply with a No. 1 brush. Once this wash has dried, I begin to add the detail.

Starting with the leaves, I carefully mark on the position of the main veins using a fine No. 000 brush and leaf green. Then I begin to shade between the veins, using sap green and leaf green, both mixed with ultramarine blue. For the smaller veins I use the tiny No. 00000 brush with Hooker's green and ultramarine blue.

Next I add the flower details, using cadmium red pale, vermilion, lemon yellow, and scarlet lake, building up tone at the base of the flower.

Turning now to the runner bean itself, I lay a wash of pale leaf green and lemon yellow, taking care to keep my brush strokes running in the direction of growth. Once this has dried I paint a darker green on top, comprising pale leaf green and ultramarine blue, leaving a strip of the lighter colour, free of shading, running down both sides of the bean. One side of the bean is slightly darker than the other, so I emphasize this by mixing a stronger combination of green and blue and applying it to the side of the bean, using a fairly fluid action and letting the colours mix together.

Notice how the runner bean is marked with thousands of fine diagonal lines, which create its texture. To achieve this I paint tiny diagonal lines in a dilute mixture of green and blue on top of the underpainting whilst it is still damp. This helps to soften the lines, whilst still allowing them to retain enough definition to give texture.

Radishes: demonstration

Original size: 22 x 25cm (8¾ x 10in)
Paper: Saunders Waterford Series, 180gsm (90lb) HP
Brushes: Nos. 1, 000, and 00000 sable

Radishes are one of the quickest and easiest vegetables to grow. They are quite delightful when freshly pulled from the garden and eaten immediately with bread and butter and a little salt. Before eating too many, however, try painting them! They make the ideal picture for the kitchen. Notice how, in contrast to many fruits and vegetables, the radish has a dull shine, rather than a bright gleaming surface.

I have divided this demonstration into four stages. The first two concentrate on the radish and the second two on the leaf formation and stems.

Stage 1

After drawing the outline of the radish very lightly with an HB pencil, I lay a transparent wash of cadmium red pale mixed with scarlet lake.

Stage 2

Once the first ground wash has dried, I gradually start building up tone and definition. To achieve the dull shine I add a lot of water to the paint, and with a circular motion of the brush I begin lifting off the paint from the paper in the areas where I wish to create a highlight. Then I define the edges of the radish by mixing the reds with purple lake and a hint of blue. For the long root hanging from each radish I use scarlet lake and brown, with the very fine hairs painted in with a No. 00000 paintbrush, and those appearing against the red background added with a little designer gouache white to make them stand out.

Stage 1

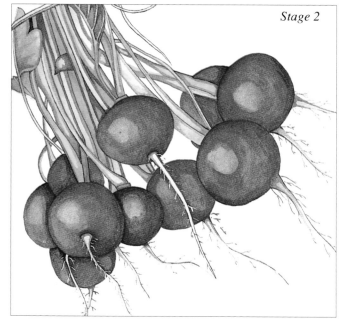

Stage 2

Stage 3

Stage 3

As for the radish, I start by drawing the outline of the leaves and stems in pencil and then lay washes of either dilute lemon yellow mixed with sap green, or dilute lemon yellow mixed with leaf green and ultramarine blue.

Stage 4

With a fine No. 00000 paintbrush I begin to define the veins in the leaves and edge them with a faint line of burnt sienna. Notice how between each vein the shading appears much darker. Here I add less water and more ultramarine blue to the greens, and apply them with a No. 000 brush.

Stage 5 – the finished painting

Now, I add the finishing touches: thin dark-green veins in the leaves and further definition of light against dark. Finally, I add a little more detail to the string to bring it to life, and I brighten the red of the radish.

Stage 4

Stage 5 – the finished painting

Sweetcorn

Original size: 10 x 33cm (4 x 13¼in)
Paper: Saunders Waterford Series, 180gsm (90lb) HP
Brushes: Nos. 3, 2, and 00000 sable

Beautifully packaged in its own wrapping, sweetcorn is a lovely-looking vegetable. As you peel back the husk the round yellow seeds are revealed, looking rather like rows of shiny teeth. Freshly picked, boiled until really golden in colour, and eaten with plenty of butter, sweetcorn is as good to eat as it is to look at!

I start this study by roughly drawing the outline of the whole structure with a soft 3B pencil. Then, with an HB pencil, I gradually form the rows of seeds, taking care to make each one appear round. Using a lemon-yellow wash I paint the seeds, leaving an area of white highlight on each one to make them look shiny and succulent. Once this is dry I shade around the edges, going over every seed carefully with spectrum yellow gouache and vermilion. Then I outline the gaps between the seeds with Vandyke brown and burnt sienna, using a No.

00000 paintbrush. This gradual building up of colour helps to make the corn really stand out from the page.

At the tip of the cob you will notice that the seeds are paler in colour. I paint these using white gouache mixed with lemon yellow, and edge them finely with a very pale mixture of sap green and ultramarine blue. Then I begin to paint the outer casing of leaves, laying a wash of white gouache, lemon yellow, and green with a larger No. 3 brush. I form the shadows using sap green, ultramarine blue, and Hooker's green, applied in such a way as to create a layered appearance. Using my smallest paintbrush, almost dry, I add fine lines along the leaves in blue, green, and brown.

I paint the stalk by adding a wash of leaf green, and for the delicate lines I use burnt sienna. To complete the painting I paint the silken tassel which escapes from the husk at the end of the corn-cob using a No. 00000 brush. Notice how the silk starts off green and then becomes brown at the ends. The tiny strands of pale silk that have been growing inside the husk are added using white gouache and a fine brush.

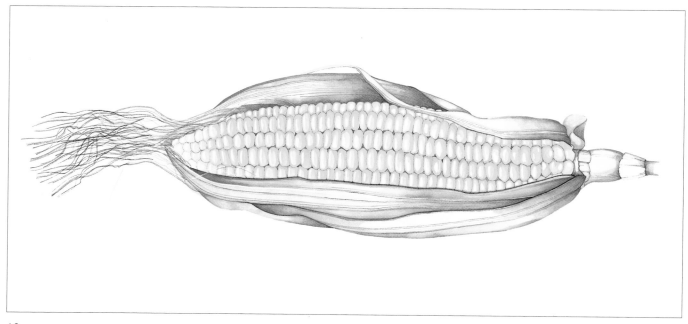

Garden pea: demonstration

Original size: 30.5 x 28cm (12¼ x 11¼in)
Paper: Saunders Waterford Series, 180gsm (90lb) HP
Brushes: Nos. 1, 000, and 00000 sable

As summer arrives, so does the garden pea, with its simple, unassuming colours and texture, and of course its succulent flavour, especially when it is picked and eaten straight from the vegetable garden.

In Stages 1 and 2 of this demonstration I have described the flowers and leaves, whilst Stages 3 and 4 show the fully grown pea-pod and pea in detail. Finally, there is the complete picture, to which I have added the Green-Veined White butterfly, which you will invariably see when you are picking peas.

Stage 1

Having first drawn in a delicate outline, I start by giving the leaves and stems a preliminary wash of sap green, lemon yellow, and ultramarine blue, using a No. 1 brush and carefully leaving the flower-heads free so that the white paper shines through.

Stage 2

Once the initial wash has dried, I start adding the details. The leaves are bluish in colour, with faint green veins running through them. To achieve this I use a fine No. 000 paintbrush, with strong mixtures of the same colours used in the underwash. The flowers are very delicate in colouring, so try not to overwork them too much. Essentially, the white of the paper forms their colour, and all that is required is a little definition. For shape and shading I use sap green mixed with Prussian blue and Vandyke brown, applied with a No. 00000 brush.

Stage 1

Stage 2

13

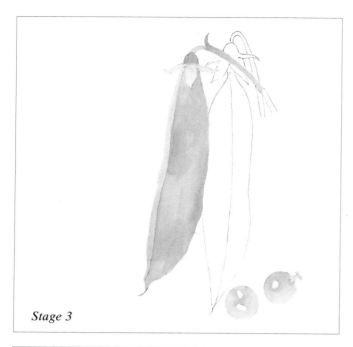

Stage 3

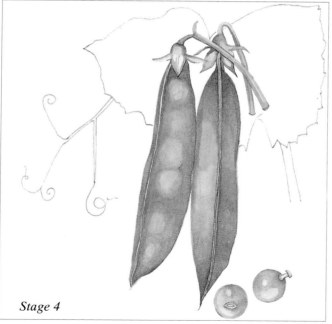

Stage 4

Stage 3

Using a sharp HB pencil, I draw the subject first before I lay the wash, which is a mixture of leaf green, sap green, and lemon yellow, again using a No. 1 brush.

Stage 4

Using plenty of dilute colour and circular movements of the brush, I form the shape of the pea inside the pod. I add the shadowed areas at the top and bottom and the edges of the pod with a mixture of ultramarine blue and Hooker's green. The sepals at the top of the pod are painted in gamboge yellow shaded with green, and outlined with Vandyke brown.

Stage 5 – the finished painting

For the final painting I simply put all four stages together and add a Green-Veined White butterfly using designer white gouache, lemon yellow, dilute sap green, and a little ultramarine blue. The pea family (*Leguminosae*) is much larger than you might think, and encompasses such plants as the sweet pea (see pages 25–7), laburnum, wistaria, runner bean (see page 8), and many others. Look at their flowers and you will see how closely related they are! Members of this family make marvellous paintings. Their nature is such that they have a natural vitality of form which translates well to paper without any need for the stilted forcing of flowers and plants into unnatural poses for the sake of composition.

Stage 5 – the finished painting

Strawberries: demonstration

Original size: 16 x 14cm (6½ x 5½in)
Paper: Saunders Waterford Series, 180gsm (90lb) HP
Brushes: Nos. 2, 1, 000, and 00000 sable

Strawberries must be one of England's most popular fruits, conjuring up visions of long, hot summer days and tea and tennis on the lawn. In complete contrast to the delicate flowers (see pages 21–2), the strawberry is large, bold, shiny, and full of brash colour.

Stage 1

After the initial pencil drawing I first paint the seeds on the strawberry with lemon yellow, using a No. 000 brush. I then lay a wash of watered-down cadmium red pale over the whole strawberry, excluding the seeds and the unripened areas, which are painted yellow or green. The stems and bracts are painted in sap green mixed with lemon yellow.

Stage 2

I deepen the red with a second wash of paint, taking care to emphasize the shape of the fruit by working ever darker washes into the shadows. The stems and bracts are shaped by adding ultramarine blue to the sap green.

Stage 1

Stage 2

Stage 3 – the finished painting

I add yet another wash of red to the fruit to darken still further the areas that need deeper shading. This is done by mixing cadmium red pale with carmine and vermilion. The lighter highlights are washed with water. I then lift off some of the excess colour with a clean brush. Once the paint is completely dry I take my finest No. 00000 brush and accentuate the outside of each seed with Vandyke brown. I use white gouache to add highlights to some of the surface dimples caused by the seeds. This gives the strawberry its shiny appearance. The leaves are painted in exactly the same way as in the picture of the strawberry flower (see pages 21–2).

Cherries: demonstration

Original size: 16 x 12.5cm (6½ x 5in)
Paper: Saunders Waterford Series, 180gsm (90lb) HP
Brushes: Nos. 2, 1, 000, and 00000 sable

These luscious dark-red cherries with their tough, shiny leaves
had to be covered with fleece as they ripened to stop the birds
eating them all.

Rather than picking the cherries and arranging them in a
bowl, I chose to leave the fruit still attached to the stalks and
branch, surrounded by leaves. The contrast of red and green
is the perfect colour scheme. As you can see, the first three
stages of the demonstration concentrate on the fruit only.

Stage 1

I start by drawing the cherries with an HB pencil and then I
lightly mark in the areas to be left as highlights.

Stage 2

The initial washes of carmine and scarlet lake are applied using
a No. 1 brush loaded with sufficient colour for each cherry.

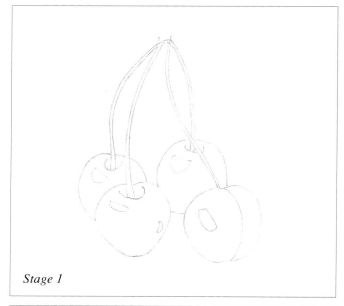

Stage 1

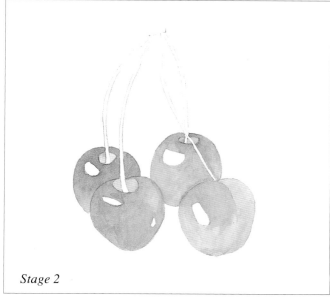

Stage 2

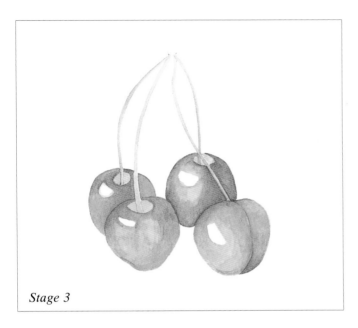

Stage 3

Stage 3

After the wash has dried, I start adding the shading and deepening the colour. Around the area left white I paint a wash of spectrum yellow. The darker shading is a mixture of carmine red and purple lake. I paint the stems with a mixture of leaf green and lemon yellow.

Stage 4 – the finished painting (overleaf)

Before each fruit is complete I start to add colour to the leaves to check that the balance of tones is correct as I go along. Firstly, I wash the leaves with sap green. Then I gradually strengthen the colour with ultramarine blue and brown, taking care to leave the first green underpainting shining through in fine lines to form the veins. The under-side of the leaf is painted using Hooker's green and blue, mixed with plenty of water to dilute the colours. Again I add the shading and veins in the same way, noting the paler colouring.

Once the leaves are complete I recheck the balance of colours, strengthening or diluting where necessary and taking care to make each fruit stand out from another or fall behind it where it should. Remember that your cherries are round – make sure that they look it.

The branch is washed first with yellow ochre. Again, notice the highlights at this stage. Details are then added with a fine No. 000 brush in burnt sienna, Vandyke brown, sap green, and a hint of ultramarine blue. Finally, when the washes are completely dry, the tiny lines and details are added in Vandyke brown and ultramarine blue, using a No. 00000 brush.

Stage 4 – the finished painting

Strawberry flower: demonstration

Original size: 18 x 26cm (7¼ x 10½in)
Paper: Saunders Waterford Series, 180gsm (90lb) HP
Brushes: Nos. 2, 1, 000, and 00000 sable

Originally I had intended painting only the strawberry plant in fruit for one of my examples in this book, but whilst watching the strawberries ripening it occurred to me just how lovely the strawberry flowers are. I then decided to do two pictures, showing the difference between the plant in flower and the plant in fruit.

Stage 1

Firstly, I draw in the flower and leaves using an HB pencil, then I lay a wash on the leaves in sap green and lemon yellow, using a No. 2 brush.

Stage 2

I begin to add form to the plant using a No. 1 brush. The white petals of the strawberry flower are achieved by leaving some of the white paper untouched, whilst the shadows are formed by mixing ultramarine blue with ivory black and lemon yellow. White is always a difficult colour to paint. Remember that white reflects all colours in the spectrum (as opposed to black, which absorbs them all), so the shadows you see are made up of colours which are reflected off its surface. Look carefully at how each petal touches another. Notice the shape and colour of the shadow which is produced and try to copy it.

Taking a No. 000 brush, I edge the stems with purple lake on one side and a darker green on the other. I gradually build up the tone of the leaves by outlining the veins and then painting a darker secondary wash of sap green mixed with ultramarine blue alongside them, sometimes adding more water to soften the effect.

Stage 1

Stage 2

Stage 3 – the finished painting

Stage 3 – the finished painting

To complete the painting of the flowers, I darken the centres, and then, with undiluted spectrum yellow gouache, I dot stamens around the flower centres. Next, I edge a number of leaves with purple lake and Vandyke brown. To create the patchwork effect of the strawberry leaves I divide the leaf into sections, using a fine No. 00000 brush. Leaving some paler undercolour showing through, I outline each section with darker ultramarine and green, adding water where necessary to soften the outlines.

Cherry blossom: demonstration

Original size: 19 x 12cm (7½ x 4¾in)
Paper: Saunders Waterford Series, 180gsm (90lb) HP
Brushes: Nos. 1, 000, and 00000 sable

My specimen of cherry blossom was picked from my garden. I chose a dry, sunny day, just as I saw the buds opening, and took great care finding exactly the right bough. I did not want to end up with all the leaves and blossom on one half of the paper, so it took time to find one along which leaves and blossom were evenly distributed. Never pick blossom after it has just rained, because you will find that the petals will quickly drop once you have taken it inside. There is nothing more frustrating than starting a picture and finding that your subject is constantly altering, with leaves and petals wilting or dying.

Stage 1

I begin my picture by faintly outlining the blossom and leaves using a sharp HB pencil.

Stage 2

Notice how the leaves are brownish in colour (umber brown with leaf green) when they start to open, quickly changing to light green as the leaves grow. Using a dilute mixture of sap green and lemon yellow, I paint the lightest side of the leaves first, later adding a hint of ultramarine blue to the green to achieve the darker colour for the shadier parts of the leaves. The branch is washed with Vandyke brown and lemon yellow. The whitest parts of the petals are untouched white paper. I carefully outline each petal with ivory black and then add the

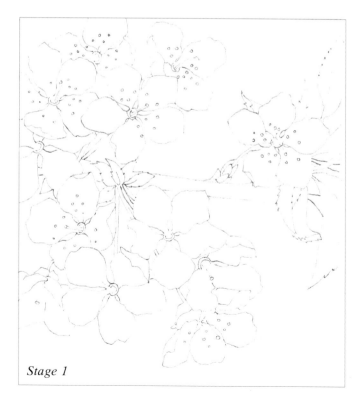

Stage 1

Stage 2

delicate shadows to the white areas using pale ivory black mixed with ultramarine blue.

Stage 3 – the finished painting

Study carefully the shading on the petals. Where the petals overlap each other I usually paint the one underneath darker to help make the petal on top stand out. I gradually build up the shading with either ivory black mixed with Prussian blue, or lemon yellow and a hint of leaf green mixed with permanent white gouache. Finally, I dot the stamens with spectrum yellow gouache, and, using a tiny No. 00000 brush, I outline each dot with a mixture of burnt sienna and brown. With the very delicate variation of colour required when painting white, one of the greatest problems is how to make the white blossom stand out from the white paper. To help with this, I add leaves behind most of the flowers. Finally, I use a small pointed brush to define the veins on the leaves and the lines on the bark.

Sweet peas: demonstration

Original size: 28 x 26cm (11¼ x 10½in)
Paper: Saunders Waterford Series, 180gsm (90lb) HP
Brushes: Nos. 2, 1, and 00000 sable

Sweet peas are one of my favourite flowers, whether I am painting them or simply looking at huge haphazard bunches of them which fill the house with their heavenly scent. I think it is the colours which appeal to me most, ranging as they do from deepest purple – almost blacl – right through the spectrum to the purest of whites. Their delicate, vein-lined blooms provide the perfect challenge for the watercolour painter. Before gathering your bunch of sweet peas, notice how they grow; how delicate and beautifully formed each flower is; how each flower joins the stem; the direction of the leaves; how blooms and stalks twist and curl; how the sun shines through their transparent, tissue-like petals with dramatic effects of colour and tone.

Stage 1

After gathering a bunch of variously coloured blooms from the garden, I spend some time studying them, noting their colour and structures carefully before deciding upon a group to paint. I start by using a sharp HB pencil, lightly drawing in my design from the centre of the picture and working gradually outwards and upwards. The natural twisting shape of the plant is a great help to composition, providing a lively, rhythmic quality. Next, I begin to lay in the first washes of transparent colour using a No. 2 brush. Choose your colour carefully, testing it out on a spare sheet of paper before putting paint to paper, and making sure that your brush is loaded with sufficient paint for each flower-head. Each colour wash is listed here and numbered on the drawing to aid identification.

1. I brush the tips of each flower with a wash of pale lemon yellow. Then I lay in a pale wash of rose madder over the flower-heads, with a hint of light blue near the base of each head.

2. Here I use a mixture of designer gouache white and pale lemon yellow and blue (see stage 2).

3. I lay a wash of rose madder mixed with purple lake and a hint of blue. Notice how stronger washes of the same colour are used at this stage to suggest form and shadow.

Stage 1

4. Using sap green and lemon yellow, I first lay a pale wash over both the buds and the leaves, adding just a hint of blue to the leaves.

5. Again, the tips of the petals are edged in pale yellow. Then I lay a wash of highly diluted purple lake and ultramarine blue.

6. With plenty of water on the brush, I use a mixture of cadmium red pale and gamboge for this delicate sweet pea.

7. Here I use the same colours as those used in flower No. 1, but with slightly more paint on the brush to give more depth to the colour.

8. Leaving the centre white, I lay in a wash of watered-down rose madder and purple lake.

9. I use a less dilute mixture of cadmium red pale. Notice the difference this makes to the watery mixture of the same colour used in flower No. 6.

The leaves and stems are washed with a delicate combination of sap green, lemon yellow, and Hooker's green.

Stage 2

Stage 3 – the finished painting

I am careful not to overwork the sweet peas, since they can easily lose their vitality. The paint needs to be so delicately and cleanly handled that the flowers' tissue-like quality is almost tangible. Too many, or heavy-handed, washes of colour could destroy their transparency. Once they reach this stage I begin to add the final details, such as veins and tiny hairs, using a fine No. 00000 brush. Notice the ridged quality of the stems, which I shade with ultramarine blue, adding tiny red lines down each stalk. For the fine hairs I use a mixture of green and red, and I brush the neck of each sweet pea where it joins the stem with Vandyke brown.

Variation – circular design

Once you have perfected the art of painting flowers it is great fun to begin to make designs with them. This example shows how adaptable the sweet pea, with its twirling tendrils and intertwined stems, can be in design work for borders and decoration.

Stage 2

I start to build up the flowers, adding different strengths of colour to define shape and form, paying particular attention to the vein shapings within petals. Some of this shading is done wet-in-wet to soften the forms and allow the colours to mingle subtly. For example, I add ultramarine blue in varying degrees to the paint mixtures to create shading on the pink and purple flowers. For the red sweet peas (No. 7), I add carmine red and a hint of purple lake. Remember that half-closing your eyes will help you to see tone when studying the flowers. This makes colour become less distinct, and it is then easier to see where the light or dark tones fall. I also take great care to shade at the bases of the petals and where the flowers overlap each other, to add definition. You will find, as in Nos. 6 and 7 or 1 and 4, for example, that it helps definition to put a pale colour behind a dark one, or vice versa.

Variation – circular design

Stage 3 – the finished painting

Mixed herbs: demonstration

Original size: 30 x 25cm (12 x 10in)
Paper: Saunders Waterford Series, 180gsm (90lb) HP
Brushes: Nos. 1, 000, and 00000 sable

Colour is the biggest challenge when painting herbs. The variations in the colour green are infinite and the great delicacy of individual plants and their varied textures are fascinating to study. Here I have picked out a few of the more popular herbs, including rosemary, with its spiky appearance; the powdery-blue/green sage; dill; chives; common thyme; golden marjoram; mint, with its dark leaves and contrasting purplish-red stem; borage; tarragon; lavender; and feverfew. All of these grow easily in any garden. As well as having culinary and medicinal benefits, they attract bees, flies, and many species of butterfly, and add wonderful scents to the garden.

Stage 1

I begin the composition by drawing the rosemary with an HB pencil. Then I add the first colours to the flowers – a mixture of carmine, ultramarine blue, and purple lake, mixed with a lot of water to

Stage 1

28

create a pale wash. The details are added using a
No. 00000 brush, with a mixture of purple lake and
blue. I paint the leaves with a wash of lemon yellow
and Hooker's green, and then edge them with a
darker green. With a fine brush I add the line details
to the stem. I wash the mint with sap green and the
underleaf in pale lemon yellow, sap green, and
white, and paint the stem with purple lake. At this
stage I draw in the sage behind the rosemary.

Stage 2

Stage 2

Now I start adding more herbs – feverfew, tarragon,
and borage. Firstly, I wash them with dilute sap
green, then later I begin to build up the shaping of
the leaves, adding darker tones and forming the
detailed veins.

Stage 3

Having drawn in all the remaining plants, I add the dill, wash the chives with sap green and ultramarine blue, and paint the lavender and borage flowers using ultramarine blue and purple lake.

Stage 3

Stage 4 – the finished painting

It is only once all the herbs have been placed on the paper that I begin to add details to all the plants: the delicate edging of brown on the rosemary leaves; the darkest tones and tiny hairs. All herbs are extremely detailed to paint and you do need to give yourself plenty of time to concentrate on each specimen. As a final touch I add a Common Blue butterfly, which complements the colour scheme perfectly.

Stage 4 – the finished painting

First published in Great Britain 1993
Search Press Limited,
Wellwood, North Farm Road,
Tunbridge Wells, Kent TN2 3DR

Text, drawings, and paintings by Kathleen Stroud
Text, illustrations, arrangement, and typography
copyright ©1993 Search Press Limited

ISBN 0 85532 746 4

Publishers' note
There are references to sable hair and other animal hair brushes in this book. It is the Publishers' custom to recommend synthetic materials as substitutes for animal products wherever possible. There are now a large number of brushes available made of artificial fibres and they are just as satisfactory as those made of natural fibres.

Distributors to the art trade:

UK
Winsor & Newton,
Whitefriars Avenue, Wealdstone,
Harrow, Middlesex HA3 5RH

USA
ColArt Americas Inc.,
11 Constitution Avenue,
P.O. Box 1396, Piscataway, NJ 08855-1396

Arthur Schwartz & Co.,
234 Meads Mountain Road, Woodstock, NY 12498

Canada
Anthes Universal Limited,
341 Heart Lake Road South, Brampton, Ontario L6W 3K8

Australia
Max A. Harrell,
P.O. Box 92, Burnley, Victoria 3121

Jasco Pty Limited,
937–941 Victoria Road, West Ryde, N.S.W. 2114

New Zealand
Caldwell Wholesale Limited,
Wellington and Auckland

South Africa
Ashley & Radmore (Pty) Limited,
P.O. Box 2794, Johannesburg 2000

Trade Winds Press (Pty) Limited,
P.O. Box 20194, Durban North 4016

Printed in Spain by A.G. Elkar, S. Coop, 48012 Bilbao